Same

Same

Poems on Love, Sisterhood and Womanhood

Hannah Rosenberg

HarperCollins*Publishers*

HarperCollins*Publishers*
1 London Bridge Street
London SE1 9GF

www.harpercollins.co.uk

HarperCollins*Publishers*
Macken House, 39/40 Mayor Street Upper
Dublin 1, D01 C9W8, Ireland

First published in the United States by St. Martin's Griffin,
an imprint of St. Martin's Publishing Group, 2026

Published in the UK by HarperCollins*Publishers*

1 3 5 7 9 10 8 6 4 2

© Hannah Napier Rosenberg Paul 2025

Designed by Gabriel Guma

Hannah Rosenberg asserts the moral right to be identified as the author of this work

A catalogue record of this book is available from the British Library

ISBN 978-0-00-873953-9

Printed and bound in the UK using 100% renewable
electricity at CPI Group (UK) Ltd

All rights reserved. No part of this publication may be reproduced,
stored in a retrieval system, or transmitted, in any form or by any means,
electronic, mechanical, photocopying, recording or otherwise,
without the prior written permission of the publishers.

Without limiting the exclusive rights of any author, contributor or the publisher of
this publication, any unauthorised use of this publication to train generative artificial
intelligence (AI) technologies is expressly prohibited. HarperCollins also exercise their
rights under Article 4(3) of the Digital Single Market Directive 2019/790 and
expressly reserve this publication from the text and data mining exception.

This book is produced from FSC™ certified paper and other controlled sources
to ensure responsible forest management.

For more information visit: www.harpercollins.co.uk/green

A Dedication, in Four Parts

To my mother and my husband. Two very different people who, with every fiber of their beings, believe in me. Thank you for helping me to believe in myself.

To Nanna and Pa, who made me feel like a star every day of my childhood. I'll never stop missing you.

To my daughter. You came to earth to live your life, but you are teaching me how to live mine.

And to my friends. My sisters, the first friends I had, and the ones I've made along the way. Wherever I go, wherever I am, there is nothing that has saved my life more than a good friend.

Contents

Introduction   xv

I. FOR OUR YOUNGER SELVES

Me as a woman, me as a girl	3
Ideas for playing house	5
Swim lessons	7
Three fingers pointing	9
When people say "we can learn from kids" and make it sound trite, cute, fake	11
My niece tells me about the first day of fourth grade.	13
The compliment game	15
Glow	17
In my daydream, our daughters are strong.	19
A bedtime story	21

At my wedding I did not feel my most beautiful. ... 23

Poem for Katie ... 25

Generational drama ... 27

Teenage girls are superheroes ... 29

II. FOR OUR FRIENDS

How we met ... 33

Tennessee ... 35

Roommates in my twenties ... 37

Once upon a time, in an apartment in Boston ... 39

Bachelorette ... 41

Group text ... 43

Women were put on earth to trust each other ... 45

Marriage of friends ... 47

Texting with friends ... 49

This is your reminder to plan a girls trip ... 51

When I needed my friends ... 53

My friends taught me ... 55

Women at a restaurant ... 57

Always at home with them ... 59

III. FOR THE ONES WE DATE AND MARRY

If we met at a dinner party in another life ... 63

When I kissed you across the table in Chinatown ... 65

With you	67
To do it, anyway	69
In the middle of the night I wake up coughing	71
In Portugal	73
A fever	75
A fight with my husband at the museum	77
And then some more	79
Married with children	81
Magic disguised as ordinary life	83
You don't write love poems but sometimes	85
In a forgettable diner, I fall in love with life	87
We got nothing done and the weekend was perfect	89

IV. FOR OUR FAMILIES

At a restaurant in the future	93
Sisters on the telephone	95
What my grandmother said	97
A poem for aunts and the people who love them	99
When I think of my ancestors	101
To the children I love	103
Type B fun	105
A visit to my sister's	107
Cycle of women	109
Opposite of generational trauma	111

Human mothers vs. insects	113
For my daughter, I would	115
In Istanbul, my daughter's hair is wild.	117
If you were here	119
Most alive	121
When we were young	123
The places I've lived are like people I love.	125

V. FOR OUR BODIES

Half-marathon	129
So I call my body "she"	131
I took my thighs to the beach.	133
Ideas for how to make gynecology appointments better	135
I want to talk to my body	137
Curls	139
Old and wild things	141
I don't know much about human biology	143

VI. FOR OUR MINDS

Turns out	147
To all of the women I've been before	149
Vulnerability is the best host	151
Maybe the things we're scared of are really our superpowers.	153
In London I learned to love myself	155

Same	157
June	159
Until I thought of myself as the sea	161
The world is unpredictable and so, often, are my moods	163
Not therapy, but it just might help	165
People who annoy us	167
(In the best of ways) no one cares what I do	169
I want ~~my child~~ to be	171
Perspective	173
Everyone on the internet has it more together than me*	175
How I want this all	177

VII. FOR OUR CHILDREN

I forgot to say thank you	181
The year I became a mother	183
My mothering mind is split in half.	185
A parent and a child	187
Need	189
New mom friends	191
Moms Group	193
Breastfeeding	195
At least once a week the plans go awry.	197
Surviving is thriving	199
A village it takes	201

Home maker	203
Little moment with little you	205
Twenty years from now I will not remember this hour	207
Meals with my daughter	209
Am I doing this right?	211
Being your mother, being your friend	213
It all, I think, comes down to friendship.	215
Acknowledgments	217

There's a lot of beauty in ordinary things.
Isn't that kind of the point?

—Pam Beesly, *The Office*

Introduction

A few years ago, I started sharing poems on the internet. Writing poetry had always been a way for me to dissect and process life, to make sense of difficult things, to stay awake to all of the joy around me amidst the monotony of the day-to-day. But I had never shared my work in such a public way before, and at first, it was mostly friends who were reading along. Friends who sent me loving messages, who commented, shared, and celebrated my writing. Friends who made me feel confident and good about something that felt so very vulnerable. Which is what friends have always done for me: They've shown up when I've been scared or worried or doing something out of my comfort zone and have supported me through it. They've listened when I've said things that have felt sensitive and raw. They've told me, *I get it. I know how you feel. Same.*

As I continued to share my work, I started hearing from people I didn't know in real life but who sounded a lot like my friends. People who were kind and generous with their own stories and feelings. Who met my vulnerability with some of their own. People who went out of their way to tell me how something I wrote made them feel seen and heard. Who told me how they sent my poem to a loved one because it helped them to celebrate that relationship, because they knew it would make that person feel understood or cared for. And that is the greatest gift I have found from sharing my writing: that sometimes, my words get to be part of the way that someone shows love—love to themselves and love to others.

Ultimately, every poem I write is some kind of love letter, and so I grouped them by relationship. Love letters for our younger selves, our friends, the ones we date and marry, our families, our bodies, our minds, our children. None of these poems are about only one type of relationship, as they're all forever overlapping, but in every loving relationship, I've found that friendship is at its core.

So, I'm sending this book of love letters out into the universe. To new friends and old, I hope that you will find yourself in these words. I hope that these words will find a home within you.

Same

I

For our younger selves

Me as a woman, me as a girl

We met the other day.
Me as a woman, me as a girl.
We looked each other up and down.
Shy at first. *It's you?* we both said, laughing.
It's you?

Me as a girl spoke first. *I like how you go
walking whenever you want. How you drink
coffee by the window and write, like I always
thought I would. I love your home,* she said,
looking around. *It feels just right.
I'd like to live here, too.*

I hoped you would, me as a woman said.
*I love your confidence. How proud you are.
How special you feel.*
Not always, me as a girl said. *Sometimes I feel sad.
Sometimes I am cruel.*
We all do. We all are, me as a woman said.

Me as a woman and me as a girl looked at each other.
*We can't exist at the same time, not exactly, but maybe
a part of me can stay with you somehow?* asked me as a girl.

Me as a woman smiled. *I'd like that,* she said.
I've been waiting my whole life to take care of someone like you.

Ideas for playing house

Your dolls wake up on a Saturday, walk out of their apartment together to get coffee and breakfast sandwiches. Return back, sit on the couch, cups in hand, turn on *Gilmore Girls*, talk about the show with the intensity of two adult women who have watched every episode multiple times. They may tell childhood stories or more recent ones—a disappointing date that week, or, perhaps a promising one, a dilemma at work or an upcoming social obligation, discuss and weigh the options back and forth. They are happy, these dolls, living with friends who also like to sit on couches and talk, who get Thai takeout on weeknights and dissect every aspect of life, who believe that what is important to one woman is important to them all. While this might not be their dollhouse forever, it is no less a home than any other they have had or will have. This is a life, not the waiting area for one, and these dolls are lucky to be living it.

Swim lessons

Remember yourself at five or seven or nine,
the way you were so ready for the world to
love everything about you. Suppose you had
never been told to look pretty or act sweet but
to fall in love with the way your hand moved
through water when you dove straight in.
How it pushed and sailed, skimmed until you
reached the surface. How you breathed in air,
gasped for it like the moment you were born.
Suppose you thought, from that very first day,
*I'll be the hero of my own story. I'll be the
one who will save my own life.*

Three fingers pointing

A friend in college once said to me
*when you talk about how you need
to lose weight, imagine how it makes me feel.*
And if I could go back in time,
back, back, back to when my mind was
first developing, I would promise to
learn that when I shame my own
body, I am shaming all women and
when I shame women, I am inviting
everyone who hears me to do the same.

When people say "we can learn from kids" and make it sound trite, cute, fake

A woman I don't know once wrote online that her young daughter described pants not fitting as her legs being too powerful and today I tried on a jumpsuit that barely fit over my hips. I thought, almost instinctively, *what powerful legs*, and for a minute in that store's dressing room as I stood with my thirty-seven-year-old body, a young girl's words did not feel cute or fake or trite at all.

My niece tells me about the first day of fourth grade.

She says there are new kids in class and I say *make sure to be kind!* Such an adult thing to say, advice without a reason, guidance without a story. She asks what she should say because she is nine and describes everything out of her comfort zone as *weird*. I get it, I've let the feeling of weird stop me from being kind, even allowed it to make me unkind, although I'm too ashamed to admit it to her eager face. Instead, I tell her about sixth grade, when I was new to a school and a girl in my class scooped me up, carried me with her. Twenty-five years later, I still feel that same sting of vulnerability when I am on the outside, still grateful when I am carried, still thankful for that child's innate kindness decades ago. *I thought of you today*, I text her, my friend still, even after so long.

The compliment game

A substitute teacher in elementary school
once told me I had a talent for writing
dialogue and over two and a half decades
later, I still think about it.
I don't remember if she said something
kind to everyone in class that day,
only that she said it to me.
We never know whose day we will change,
whose life will be impacted by our words.
The lesson, I think? Give compliments
wherever you go. Children need them to
grow and adults are just older children,
waiting for someone to notice all of the
ways that they are good.

Glow

Growing up at the turn of the century
there were legendary stories about
girls being "discovered."
Walking in malls, singing in church,
kicking a soccer ball in school.
It is true, there is nothing in life we can do
alone. And yet, what if the moral of the story
wasn't that you could be so lucky to have
someone else notice your glow, but that you
might—and you *would*—discover it all on your own.

In my daydream, our daughters are strong.

They learn words like *capable, confident, resilient.*
They aren't taught to be careful in ways you
are careful with a vase because it is fragile.
Something meant to look at. Something you
might break. They are careful like how you are
careful with something you love. Something that
makes you proud. They don't worry that they
have too many needs or take up too much space.
They don't wonder if they are small enough or liked
enough. They wonder about the world and how to
make it better. How to soak up all the good in life.
They ask each other: *What makes your heart sing?*
They talk of their own courage. They lead with joy.

A bedtime story

Every time I buy myself an ice cream cone
on a Tuesday,
take myself out to lunch on a Wednesday,
get two entrees to eat alone, read a book in bed,
watch a television show that delights me,
take a long shower, a long nap,
take myself to the doctor, hold my own hand
in a cold, sterile room, take care of myself in
a way that feels tender and warm,
I think about how every child should be told a story
about how they may be their own villain, their own
monster, their own evil queen,
but in the end, they will become a hero.
Even in a simple, ordinary life,
they will be the hero of their own.

At my wedding I did not feel my most beautiful.

The dress was nice but not my favorite I'd ever worn.
My hair did not turn out the way I had imagined.
Plus, it rained. In the end, none of it mattered much, anyway.
I laughed until I cried mascara tears, picked up my nieces,
swung them around, jumped up and down with my
brand-new husband and our favorite people,
danced and danced and danced until sweat became me.

After the wedding, a friend told me I was the happiest bride
she had ever seen. And even though I have thought for
so long about how to be pretty, about how to be a pretty bride,
if I had to choose between the two, happy is what I would
choose every time.

Poem for Katie

We drew our dream weddings,
circled boys in the yearbook we
thought were cute. Devised plans
to make them fall in love with us.
Stared out the window to wait
for the handsome neighbor to appear.
Wrote notes back and forth. *What did he say?*
What does that mean? What should I do?
And all the while, we laughed at
each other's jokes, wrote our own
language, collected details about
the other and memorized them,
like you do when something matters.
Now we have daughters of our own,
and the only love I wish for them as
they grow is the kind that comes
with a friend like you.

Generational drama

I'm starting to think my one-year-old daughter
might have inherited my dramatic gene.
We both dance when no one is watching,
but prefer when people are.
We involve my husband, her father, in
make-believe scenarios every day just so
we all can laugh. We laugh loudly, often at ourselves,
cry in public regularly too, no problem there.
We both love singing in the car, music blaring,
our voices ablaze.

It's fun to see part of myself in her, but the best
thing about starting to see this gene repeat itself?
I can teach her that she is a light,
and that she doesn't have to dim herself
for anyone.

Teenage girls are superheroes

Half of a high school identification card,
the half with my sixteen-year-old face on it,
leans against a picture frame on my desk.
It feels inconceivable that while I am sitting
here in my thirties, that girl isn't still a teenager,
going to school every day, living in her childhood home.
It feels unbelievable that the girl is me.
Or, maybe, that I am the girl.
Hey, I say. *Hey*, she says.
I want to tell her what I've done.
That I am doing what she's always dreamed of.
That I have a family of my own.
That, no, we've not figured it all out, but really no one has,
and learning that was so much better.
But I guess she knows that. It's what she's done, she's learned.
I want to tell her about all the people I've met,
all the friends I've made, the ones I've kept,
but she is the one who's met and kept all of these people, too.
I want to tell her this so that she can be proud of who she is,
but I think, actually, she already was.
The thing about teenage girls is that even amidst the
angst of young personhood, they are brave and strong and whole.
They do not need the world to save them.
They do not need to be saved at all.
They can save themselves just fine,
while becoming whoever they want to be.

II

For our friends

How we met

We met in school, in class, in a dorm,
on the field, at a party, in a book club,
at high tea in London. We met on a rooftop,
in a bar, at work, in line, through marriage,
through friends, through friends, through
friends. I used to always wonder how I'd
meet my husband, not knowing that there
would be so many little love stories about
how I met my friends.

Tennessee

In Nashville, we lived together in small dorms,
cramped rooms with little space to breathe.
The city was ours, or that's how we felt,
going out into the world at night, young women
certain of nothing except that we belonged together.
There's a saying that life happens while you're
making other plans. While we were planning for
what we thought would be the end of school and
beginning of everything else, our lives were happening
before us. I can't tell you how many things I learned
in college, but one of them was that life is better
when you have friends that become a family,
that make any place feel like home.

Roommates in my twenties

Before I married and mothered I lived with women.
Roommates, but that's not the right word.
We were together when we figured out who we were.
How to love who we had always been.
Each day spent under the same roof,
building a life we knew was fleeting.
How do you name a love like that?
Devotion despite impermanence.
Who sings that song?
The one that captures the days we
spent as each other's keepers,
the hours we witnessed one another
becoming.
What words can tell what ordinary,
remarkable days those were.

Once upon a time, in an apartment in Boston

Once upon a time, in an apartment in Boston,
women in their twenties gathered each month.
They made pasta and alfredo sauce, brought chips
and dips, wine, cheese, takeout containers of curries and rice.
They sat on sofas and in chairs, sprawled out on the floor,
wrapped themselves in blankets in the winter, opened up
old bay windows in the spring. They called it a book club
and talked about the book, and then they talked about other
things. Things that the book made them think of or things
that made them think of the book, the book and their lives
intertwining as books and life so often do. They talked and
talked and listened and listened and fell into deep friendship
with each other, friendship that only happens when people talk
and listen with such intention. I don't know how this story ends
and maybe it never does. Only that I was there and that for
the rest of my life, I will continue to search and to seek out the
feeling of being in a room of women who talk and listen, listen
and talk to each other.

Bachelorette

What's said at bachelorette parties:
*Let's go dancing, let's do brunch,
should we get pedicures, sit by the pool,
split margaritas, plan a hike?*

*Are you excited? Are you ready?
Can we see the dress?*

What's not said: *Marriage is beautiful,
marriage is hard. We will be here every
step of the way. You are ours for life, too.
We are yours.*

Group text

Remember when you would send a group text
on Wednesdays at 4 PM? *Anyone want to get
drinks / dinner / yoga / see a comedy show?*
Or on Saturday mornings, I'd write:
*who's free for coffee / a walk / lunch /
to hang out and watch movies on the couch all day?*

Now we say:
*how are you / I miss you /
let's catch up soon.*

*Girls trip this fall? / trip with our families
this winter? / I think I'll be in town for
work in the spring.*

Our lives look so different. I miss the
old one and still, am so happy. You get it,
I know you're the same. But in case you forgot,
I wanted to say:
*That time was the best / how lucky we were /
I love you.*

Women were put on earth to trust each other

One friend I met the first day of college, when we were placed as roommates in a dorm that barely fit us both. Two girls left for the first time to care for ourselves, spiraling in and out of chaos, holding space for each other with tender mercy. The kindness felt like an intangible home.

One friend I met in London, she and I from opposite sides of the States. We watched American sitcoms and talked of ex-boyfriends, slept for a week on opposite sides of a small double bed.

One friend I met on a student housing site. We chose different places to live but met for tea anyway, both of us far from home and deciding, quickly, to depend on each other.

One friend I met through another friend during a weekend in Montreal. We drove through Vermont and over the border, walked cobblestone streets, held umbrellas over each other's heads in early spring rain.

One friend I met again on a city sidewalk years after we had lost touch. We picked up where we had left off in childhood, thanked our lucky stars that something like fate had brought us back together.

These stories could go on and on. Stories about how I've met women and instantly, instinctively trusted them. How I've so often thought, or known without thinking at all,

I bet I could rely on you. I bet, even with all of the bad things that happen in the world, you understand what I understand. I bet I could trust you with my life.

Marriage of friends

My life is filled with the souls of women
I love. The ones who make my belly ache
from laughter, the ones who catch my tears.
Who show up on my doorstep to celebrate
and grieve, who stand up for me when I put
myself down. Women who will love my
children, dance as we age, protect my secrets,
share in my joy, sing even when we're sinking
in sorrow. They walk close, promising their
lives to me—a marriage without a wedding;
a commitment without a ring. If you have these
women, remember: the soulmate is a wonderful
thought, but look how beautiful these love
stories are. Look how they make you full.

Texting with friends

I do not live within shouting distance
of my closest friends, but our lives
intertwine on my phone. While they're
living their lives and I'm living mine.
Life comes with so many questions,
demands, bids for guilt. So many *shoulds*.
Always good news and bad news to share,
so I text my friends. And there they all are.
Not one tells me to try harder or give myself
less grace. Not one fails to make me laugh,
to remind me how I am loved. My best friends
cannot run to my house with a bag of sugar,
but they are there, across the line, telling me
that if that's what I need, they will have it
delivered straight to my door.

This is your reminder to plan a girls trip

We start the day with coffee. With questions, stories,
the beginning of what has happened since we've been
together last. We eat a slow breakfast, share pancakes,
potatoes, eggs. We park ourselves at a pool, or maybe
wander in and out of stores, go on a hike or book
appointments at a spa, sit in matching robes.
It doesn't matter where, exactly, we are, but that
we are women in friendship. What was started over
coffee is continued, woven throughout the day.
We relax in the afternoon, our bodies sprawled across
pool chairs, hotel beds, couches in rented homes.
We shower and dress for dinner, go out into the night,
drink wine and cocktails, share appetizers, split pasta
and dumplings. And after, we try to keep our eyes
open long enough to finish the stories we started.
We never do, of course, because they have no end.
We board flights or get in cars, wave goodbye and promise
to see each other soon. And when we're asked how it was,
we use words like *fun* and *great* because it is hard to describe
how good it feels to be part of a group of women who
belong to each other.

When I needed my friends

When I was younger, on every birthday,
when I was in school, when I took a job,
quit a job, moved cities, moved to another
country, moved back home, went on dates,
started a relationship, ended a relationship.
When I sought out a therapist, went to a doctor's
appointment, looked for a dress to wear.
When I moved in with a boyfriend,
got engaged, got married, had a baby.
When I healed, when I mothered, when I
thought of something funny, when I thought
of something sad, when I worried, when I
wanted to celebrate, when I had a question,
when I needed to make a decision, when I
needed to cry. On every day of the week,
week of the year, year of my life.
When I was younger, as I got older, every day,
I have needed my friends.

My friends taught me

to greet little wins with big celebrations, to greet disappointment with the same. Any news deserves a dinner out or good takeout and snacks or dancing to live music by the water. Reminding me that the good in life does not depend on if I win or lose, but whether we can spend it together.

Women at a restaurant

There's a group of us, maybe four, five, six.
We slide into a booth or into our own chairs,
pull ourselves close to the table. We open menus,
scan them for drinks. *Any starters?* the waiter asks
and we say *please!* We are eager for good food, so we
order plenty—savory, bready, anything that can be
dipped in sauce. The drinks arrive, plates are
placed on the table and we scoot in closer, arms
touching as we begin to eat. Someone asks a question,
and we dive in, listen closely as stories are told.

Have you ever been made to feel that your life, just as it is,
is not poetry? That your words are not art, that eating
isn't beautiful? I'm here to tell you it is, that it is divine
that which happens among women as they sit around
a table, as they enjoy food together, as they talk about
all of the things that make up their lives.

Always at home with them

When I'm feeling out of place or awkward, it's nice to know
I have friends who I can call, no matter how many miles away,
and say things like *Hi. What are you up to? What did you eat for lunch?
What will you watch on TV tonight?* It's nice to know I can text
them where I am, what I'm doing, what questions are going
through my mind.

It's nice to know there are people out there, even if they are not
where I am, who are happy to hear from me, who will tell me about
their own lives, who will be a witness to my own. People who make it
known that, even if I do not feel at home everywhere, I am always
at home with them.

III

For the ones we date and marry

If we met at a dinner party in another life

If we met at a dinner party in another life,
were seated next to each other around a
crowded table, distracted by food and
conversation, would we know that this life exists?
Would the way you said *hello* or the sound of my
laugh or how you picked up your fork make us pause?
Would a story you told or how I asked you
hundreds of questions make us wonder if, perhaps,
we had met before? That in another life, we did
meet and marry and have a baby, plan for more,
our lives intertwined in irreversible ways.
Would we know the hours and days we spent talking,
the years we spent sleeping in the same bed?
Would I know your face is what I would see the
moment before we met our daughter,
her small body pulled from mine?
Would we know that at restaurants, we would bounce
her back and forth, say *you eat first* when
our meals were served?
Or, not?
If we were seated next to each other at a dinner party
in another life, would we just be two strangers who briefly met?
Would, at the end of the night, you wave goodbye
as I walked outside to go home to my life, you to yours,
not knowing that in this one, we belong together.

When I kissed you across the table in Chinatown

waved goodbye as you stood on your Brooklyn stoop.
When we said *well, neither of us has plans to move,*
when you did move, after all,
when we first lived together, argued over bathroom towels,
the wrong time for dinner, the right way to fight.
When we married, thought we had figured it all out.
When we became the kind of together that feels like we'd always been.
When we had a baby and our orbits moved.
I did not know that every day I would wake up to someone
both familiar and new.
That every day we would place more puzzle pieces
on a board that would never, to our very last day, be complete.

With you

In Austin we wandered around a dry winter
in a mid-pandemic haze wondering if we would
make it to the other side of our dreams.
Dreams where we became a family, where work
was our own. We're here now, still dreaming,
and happy. But I was even then. Always happy
when I'm walking with coffee in one hand,
your hand in the other, dreaming of the future,
with you.

To do it, anyway

You are not my everything.
I rise with the sun, not you, and sometimes not even then.
You come to me on those slow mornings,
my eyelids holding the tail end of dreams.
You crouch beside my pillow, your face the
first thing I see.
Still, you are not my everything.
If I were to leave one day, you'd get on with it.
And so would I, if one day you found this life wasn't for you.
Some might say this isn't love,
but what could be more?
To give and take without guarantee?
To search for your face each morning,
knowing it might not be forever and
even forever isn't that long.
To do it, anyway.

In the middle of the night I wake up coughing

and run to the toilet. My husband follows behind. *What's wrong?* he asks, rubbing my back. *Heartburn* I say, referencing the small book that sits on our bedside table, the one that explains what is happening to my body as a tiny human grows inside. *Heartburn* he agrees, my husband who does not like vomit, who is a closed bathroom kind of person while I am an open one, one with few boundaries, body or otherwise.

We get back in bed and he kisses my belly and then my arm and I am convinced that love does not grow when they say it does. Not on sunny mornings, not in wedding gowns, not on first or second dates when we say clever things and our youthful skin parades, but at three AM when my eyes water, when I hunch over the toilet, his hand on my back, both of us wishing we weren't there and happy that we are, when he's telling me *it's okay, it's okay, it will all be okay.*

In Portugal

In Portugal we walked porcelain streets,
ate long, slow meals. You drank wine,
and I drank water, enough for both of us,
the baby and me. Each photo we took
I said *get the baby, too*, meaning my belly,
of course. How could we have known then
the depths our hearts would travel?
How could we have known once we're there
we'd never quite come back?
In Portugal, we swam, walked steep hills,
your hand in mine, and thought of a future
that was hard to imagine.
In Portugal, the baby kicked as I slept
in a European bed. The two of us, four
hands on my belly. Just months before
we were three.

A fever

After midnight, my daughter stirs, wanting to nurse.
Her skin is hot when I lean down to kiss her forehead.
I wake my husband who is sleeping beside us.
I think she has a fever, I say, and he leans over,
feels the top of her head. I hold her as he gives her
Tylenol, asks her permission.
She is new to the world of *Yeses* and *Nos*.
Yes, she says. She rests her head on my body
and he lies down beside us. *Wake me up
if she doesn't sleep*, he says and after nearly an hour
of tossing and turning, I do. The fever is gone,
but she is restless now, awake to the world.
He picks her up and they walk down the hall.
I lay my head back down, hear him open
a book, begin to read.
My husband and I have found ourselves in the net
of early parenthood. So many things feel like a fight
when they are not, like we are on two sides of a court,
when there is no game to be played.
But there are also nights like this, when we are our
own universe, our family of three, when there is nothing
and no one else in the world, when we are all thinking of
everything that we can do for each other.

A fight with my husband at the museum

The subject, like most, was forgettable.
Less about the what and more
about how we felt. Tired, slighted,
misunderstood. Alone in a feeling when we
wanted to be together. But we had parked
and our baby was awake from her nap
so we got out of the car and you took her
to one side of the museum, the side with nature
and history. *I'll look at the art* I said, waving to
you both, and took the elevator to the floor above.
I walked into galleries with paintings and sculptures,
felt hot tears sting my eyes because museums can
be sad, and life can be, too, even when nothing is wrong.
I sat on benches and stared at murals and used
the bathroom and scrolled through my phone and
eventually, walked to the side of the museum you were on.
I walked all around hoping to run into you.
I didn't, but then you called and said *we're by the bears, third floor,*
and I hurried there, found you both, our daughter making a *shushing*
sound you had taught her. You told me everything she had
done in the hour I was away, both of us delighted because she
was ours and maybe also because we were each other's.
I held our daughter and kissed you and you shared what you
had learned in the exhibit, so excited to tell me like you always are,
and I felt like crying again because even when moods are bad,
when feelings are hurt, when you go on your own way,
your people are your people, and they will always welcome
you back when you come running home.

And then some more

In twenty years I don't think we will remember
if the dishes were done or the laundry was folded
each week. Who did what percent of the housekeeping
or yard cleaning. I'm not sure we'll remember
what strategy we chose to pursue for independent
play or if we calmly agreed on the right way to
address toddler tantrums. I'll remember this
morning, I think, when we curled up in bed,
showered our daughter with morning kisses,
all of us laughing together. Not that the house
was messy or our lives disorganized or that we
hadn't figured out the best way to be the best parents.
Just that you and I gave all of the love we had to her
and to each other. All the love we thought we had,
and then some more.

Married with children

We argue mostly about time because
there is so little of it and we can't make more.
We want to be everything, do it all.

We want time to exercise, evenings out with friends,
quality time with our daughter. We want dream careers,
a clean house, to go for walks alone and together,
to sit in front of the television with no one to ask us how
long we'll be watching. And to be good partners.
We argue about the lack of time to do that, too.

It's hard to believe, sometimes, that we won't always feel this
tension of who has time to do what. But today, I said *I'll work
for an hour?* and you said *sure*, and as I sat with my laptop on the
bed I heard you in the other room, giving our daughter an
afternoon bath because we had been in the hot sun.
I heard you call it a *water adventure*, heard her giggles,
heard your make-believe voice as she splashed water toys,
heard her respond to your joy with some of her own,
and I know we will keep arguing about time for years to come
but in this moment I could hardly believe that I get to spend
the little time I have on this earth with you.

Magic disguised as ordinary life

I sit at my desk, late afternoon light in the window beside me.
You are with our daughter in the other room and I hear your
voices singing together. What a tragedy, these exceptional
things we so often ignore. Two years ago, when I wanted you
to be a father and me a mother, this would have felt like magic.
And now, so ordinary, that I almost take it for granted.
So ordinary that I almost, very nearly, let it pass me by.

You don't write love poems but sometimes

you offer me a bite even though
I should have ordered my own.
You offer to share the whole thing.
You say the jokes I like just so
I will laugh, you reach for my
hand in the car, hold it as you drive.
You're more excited for me than even
I am, you say *wherever you want to go*
for dinner, whatever you want to watch.
You say *whenever you're happy,*
that's when I'm the happiest, too.

In a forgettable diner, I fall in love with life

This week feels mundane and I wonder
how much of life I have tried to wish
away. *Three more days until the weekend.*
Two more months before the sweet relief of spring.
I complain to complain, sit in front of
two screens, hold one more to my face
and scroll through lives that promise
what looks like exhausting glamor.
But in a long line of groundhog days I
find myself with you. Sitting across from
each other at a diner with our usual order.
Our regular eggs, our shared pancakes,
talking about everything and nothing and
it feels like ordinary magic that we're here,
together, if only for a few short moments
in the endless eons of time.

We got nothing done and the weekend was perfect

By Monday morning, we've barely made a dent in our weekend tasks. Things still need fixed, errands run, clothes put away, problems solved. Each weekend, we make a list and check off boxes until the human instinct to enjoy kicks in. Then we relax, go outside, find coffee shops and ice cream stands, pop-up markets, walking trails. We visit parks and diners, say *yes* when invited to experience the world around us. At the end, we're full and happy and left with a long list, a lingering lie that maybe we should have delayed living until work was done. Only, we never do. And what a beautiful thing that is. To be so human that despite responsibility and often logic, we reach so desperately for joy.

IV

For our families

At a restaurant in the future

One evening in the future we will sit down at a restaurant
with our daughter. Perhaps another child, too.
We will order food and all pick up our own silverware.
Our children will not sit on our laps, except maybe,
if we plead with them. *Please!* we'll say, *for a picture?*
And when they comply, we'll close our eyes for a second,
breathe in the smell of their near adult heads.
I imagine they will smell to us as sweet as they do today.
We will carry on a conversation, all of us. Forks and food
will not be thrown on the floor. We will not have to apologize
to our waiter for the mess, we will not take turns walking
around the restaurant while the other one eats, we will not
shovel our food down as quickly as we can, we will not,
eventually, open our cell phones to a children's show.
We will eat slowly, listen to each other and laugh,
maybe even share a bottle of wine. Near the end of dinner,
our children will check the time. They will ask if it's okay to
leave a little early, they have other plans, and we will say *sure!*,
proud of the lives they have away from us and still, wanting to
spend as much time with them as we can. They will get up,
kiss our cheeks, walk away into the evening light and you and I
will look across the table at each other. We will smile and finish
our meal, retelling old stories, our favorite stories,
all of the stories that are happening now.

Sisters on the telephone

I called you yesterday and we fought
back and forth, each of us stubborn and firm.
We hung up in a fury but today we forgot.
Then I called and we laughed back and
forth about your babies or mine.
What they said or did, something so
normal that no one would listen but us.
You called with advice and I argued against it
but then I called back for more.
You called earlier and had nothing to say
so I walked to the store while you answered
an email and then I continued with my day.
I nearly forgot you were on the phone
and just as I was about to hang up I said
are you still there?
You said *I am.*

What my grandmother said

My grandmother never knew the boy
I met on a dance floor nearly a decade ago.
She died soon after the night that we met,
before he and I dated, lived together,
played house, moved and moved again.
Before we had a daughter that shares her middle name.
Before we spent hours and days at coffee shops,
on car rides, in conversation, in argument,
in mundane life, in love.
She never met the boy I married, but perhaps
in another universe, she did.
Perhaps near the end, things become clear.
Maybe that's why she told me, not long before she died,
to *find a dance floor*, to *go out dancing*, to meet someone
who *loved to dance but not to drink*, someone who,
even after the party was over, would sing with me
all the way home.

A poem for aunts and the people who love them

My niece likes me to tell a story
about her birth.
I was at the hospital, I say,
I wanted to meet you first.
She smiles.
*I ran past everyone to get to the room
where you were born. Where Mom had
just given birth to you.*
You ran past everyone! she squeals.
Her younger sister wants the same story
so I tell her how I was there when she was born, too.
That it's true, I wanted to be the first to meet her.
My nieces, both young, love a story that might
not always mean much to them.
Me, eager to tell it while it does.
A story of how we come into the world,
desperate to be wanted.
A story of how we stay that way.

When I think of my ancestors

I wonder if the least I can do is let
my curly hair be. Shout my name
from the rooftops, live a life I enjoy.
Tell my story and be proud of it,
all of the grit and dirt, every last flaw.
What do they care about the mirage
of perfection when the reason I'm
here is because of all they endured?
What can I do other than to honor
exactly what perseverance got them?
A lineage of people who are who they
are, and so damn proud of it, too.

To the children I love

How many mistakes have I made?
So many, over and over.
I've said the wrong words,
done the wrong things. Things I'm
ashamed of. I've hurt people when
I felt hurt, have used kindness to my
advantage. I've punished my body
just for being her. And even then,
even then, I was loved, endlessly, by
so many people. By my body, herself.
I want to say this to relieve you
of expectation. You will make mistakes,
many of them, so many of them.
You will be loved, endlessly, too.

Type B fun

Type B fun, my sister-in-law says,
is a different kind, like staying up
all night studying for medical
school exams with friends.
Right, I think, like taking six children
out to dinner on a family vacation.
Like a four-hour car ride that becomes
eight, pulling over in towns you've never
heard of to find a park.
Like singing twenty rounds of "Old MacDonald"
with your husband to keep the baby
entertained, thinking of every animal you
can so the song never ends.
Like stopping every five minutes
on a bike ride so the young people
with you can adjust their gears.
Like realizing that magic does
exist in childhood, after all.
Like realizing the magic is you.

A visit to my sister's

At my sister's, we say we'll watch a show when the kids go to sleep.
When we say we'll do it, I think maybe we've forgotten we have
children, and that these children will be with us. We say it, anyway,
even when all signs point to the fact that we will not.

One night, we start a conversation in the kitchen as we're preparing
dinner but it's interrupted when we need to feed the children the
dinner we've prepared.

One night, we pour wine in cups and bring cookies to the patio,
sit in the late evening air until a few minutes later, the sound of my
daughter's voice comes through the baby monitor.

Each day comes and goes and each child has a different bedtime,
requires different things like nursing or sitting or long
conversations.

One night, one child requires a plate of nachos at nine PM
and my sister and I both fall asleep on the couch as she is
eating them.

We never watch that show, we don't even turn on the
television. But it doesn't matter, not as much as the promise of
it, and the promise that we will always, even as we grow old,
agree that little sounds as nice as sitting on the couch
and watching television together.

Cycle of women

I go to the beach with my aunt, my sister, my cousin, her wife, our daughters. At the beach, we hold our babies as they sleep. We watch them play nearby in the sand, we walk them down to the ocean to collect water in their pails. My aunt stretches out on a towel, cheeks to the sun, back to the sky, reminding me of myself as a child, decades earlier, of my own eyes closing in the sun while my mother and aunt kept careful watch on us all. I think of what a gift it is to be part of a cycle of women who care. Who are cared for, who take care of their young and each other, who know how to care well for themselves.

Opposite of generational trauma

At my mother's house the summer
my daughter is one, she wakes up
to her cousins around her.
Figuratively and literally.
They are there, together, all week,
but also, she is aware now that they
are people, people she might love.
These cousins equal parts dote on
and ignore her in a way that shows how
love does not need pageantry.
There are so many things we pass down,
things out of our control, whether we like it or not.
And then, your sisters have children and you
have children and these children all love
each other, and I wonder if this is a kind of
inheritance too, this love that feels like a
generational gift.

Human mothers vs. insects

In August, I spend a weekend obsessed with mosquitos.
Eliminating their existence in the same space as my daughter.
In the news, there are sensationalized stories of a rare and
dangerous virus and something I had never much thought
about before consumes me. It reminds me of a summer thirty
years ago when my mother stayed up all night on a trip to
Vermont, three children in tow. A night she couldn't sleep
because flies were swarming around us under a hot summer moon.
My mother, awake, swatting them away. The story, family humor,
looks different now, when I am no longer the child being protected
from a distant and unlikely danger but the mother protecting from one.
When vigilance feels less superfluous and more necessary.
When I, too, would do everything and anything to protect my baby.
I get it now. To protect my baby, I would do it all.

For my daughter, I would

stand up to my bullies, even if the bully was me.
Work each day to make life feel brighter.
Face my demons. Learn to be stronger than
the things I am scared of.
Choose joy even when I feel angry,
jealous, slighted and small.
Love myself because I want her to
love herself too.
Try, try, try.
For my daughter, I would do all of these things.
Only now do I realize how my mother must
have done them for me.

In Istanbul, my daughter's hair is wild.

Matted after sleep, curls on fire in the sun.
For the first time in decades, I leave my curls be
on vacation, don't iron them straight. *In solidarity,*
I say to my husband as a joke, *so she's not the only one.*
And how, with so much of life, this is both funny
and deep. *My daughter*, I laugh, *your wild hair.*
My daughter, who came to earth to live her own life,
but in so many ways, is teaching me how to live mine.

If you were here

If you were here, I'd invite you for coffee.
We'd sit at my kitchen table and I'd put out
snacks, more than we both could eat and
you'd say *this is too much*, but in a way that
made me feel good. I'd ask you to tell me
about becoming a mother again, ask you about
details I didn't think of before. I didn't think of
so many things, and it all hits differently now,
you being a mother, you being my grandmother,
now that I have a baby of my own. Now that I have
a baby who shares your middle name, I wish like I've
always wished that life let you live more,
that life would let us all live more even though you
said that death was nothing to be scared of.
How do we give away our hearts to the people we love
and still make sure they stay whole?

Is there a way? I'd ask you, if you were here.

Most alive

I rarely think about the last time I
saw my grandmother alive. Instead,
I think about the times I saw her
most alive. Head thrown back in
laughter, glass of sherry in her hand.
Dancing in a nightgown, storytelling
to great applause.

Do not lose yourself in the doorway
of an empty house, memorizing
shadows as you wait to mourn.
Instead, remember the house when
it was your home. Full of spirit,
electric with life.

When we were young

My husband's mom lost her own when she was young.
All her life, she tells me, she's been searching for something
that feels like a mother. Even now, she says, even when she
has a grandchild of her own. I think about the things that
I wanted as a girl, how I try to find them now, how it seems
that despite what I thought, I'm not really moving away from
who I once was and what I once wanted. Instead, I think,
we all move closer and closer, closer and closer, until
we find ourselves again almost exactly as we were when
we were young.

The places I've lived are like people I love.

Making me think that all our significant
relationships in life don't need to be mammals.
Cities have heartbeats, towns and villages
have a soul. The coffee shops, the streets
I call home, my favorite Friday night restaurants.
The sidewalks, the trees I don't notice
until I do, the places I jog, the benches
I sit on, the water I used to look at every day.
In the end, I'll take pieces of these places with me.
In the end, I hope these places will keep pieces of me, too.

V

For our bodies

Half-marathon

When I'm thirty-six, I sign up for a half-marathon.
The year after I give birth, the year my body
becomes a tool to keep another human alive.
I start with short runs, listen to books to pass
the time. When the runs become longer, I adjust
my body and mind. Reject sinking guilt of hours
spent just for me. I practice asking my body
what it needs. I try phrases like *please enjoy.*
This fresh air, this sunlight, this relief of the
downhill. I try to say *this is not a competition.*
You are not being judged. I try to say *thank you.*
To say *after all that you've done for me, can I do this*
for you? For you, my body, my one home that will
always and only be mine.

So I call my body "she"

In all the versions of my life I cannot promise
I would have chosen her. So many bodies with
parts that run better, see better, grow better,
look better. I cannot swear I would have picked her
which makes me ache when I think that all she
does, she does for me. She knows what fear and
grief and love and good feel like. She holds them
all, in my spirit, in my bones. And when I say
can you change just a little bit more or *you've failed
me once again*, she says *it's okay. It's okay, we'll try
again tomorrow. It's okay, we'll keep on trying,
keep on trying until you and I become the earth,
until the day that you and I return to earth again.*

I took my thighs to the beach.

They asked if they could feel the salt water,
wade in the tide, jump in the sea. *Sure*, I said.
They asked if they could stretch out in the sun,
if I could sift sand through my fingers, let it fall
on them. *Sure*, I said. They asked if they could
be in a picture, just as they were, and when I
hesitated, they winced. *I'm sorry*, they said,
for what we are not. And it broke my heart for
my thighs, who want such little things,
like sand and sun, warmth and water,
but who want nothing more than to make
me feel strong and free.

Ideas for how to make gynecology appointments better

The patient walks into the room where the doctor's sitting.
Hey, the patient says to the doctor, *thanks for waiting!*
Instead of elevator music, they play The Chicks,
Beyoncé, Alicia Keys. You control the volume.
The doctor asks you to bring a picture of yourself and thumbtack
it to the wall. In the first order of business, you are
instructed to shout affirmations at the picture.
Suggestions include: *You are incredible. You are my hero.*
Is there anything you can't do?
Before asking your age, your weight, the date of your
last menstrual cycle, they ask you to tell them what you
love about your body, how it makes you feel strong.
Sometimes they ask you to describe your dream vacation,
the best meal you've ever had.
When they tell you to put your feet in the stirrups, they
say, *your body is badass. Nothing in this exam could convince*
us otherwise. They read you this poem.

I want to talk to my body

like she's a child. When she is tired,
to say *take a nap, sweetie.*
To ask if she's hungry, to find joy
in making her meals.
To slowly chop vegetables, boil noodles,
butter bread. *Here*, I want to say,
sit down. Eat.
To feel proud when she's full,
to know that food I made fed a body
I love. I want to be gentle with her.
To take time to wash her hair, to comb it.
To say *honey it's okay to cry.* I want to treat
my body like a child who is deserving of time,
of patience, of love.
Because I was. Because I am.

Curls

Of course they were born with me,
and like everything and everyone
to exist, had so very little to do
with how they came into the world.
They were what they were.

And at first, I barely gave them thought
one way or the other. Then, as I grew,
I even liked them, the way they fell from my head,
the ringlets I wrapped around my fingers,
the way others sometimes commented how nice they looked.

Until one day I decided they had to be changed.
And so I held hot irons to my head, flattened and
melted them until they did not look like themselves at all.

How confused they must have been, how awful
it would feel to be bullied into changing day after day.

And now, almost three decades later, I see the same
curls on my daughter's head, the same baby curls
coming into the world with such joy and delight and
all I want is for them to be able to live a life where
they're never told to be anything other than what they are.

Old and wild things

Isn't it true that we love the look of exposed brick,
the uneven nature of cobblestone roads?
Haven't we all stopped to take pictures of buildings
with vines climbing their sides, stood in awe of
wildflowers peppering open fields?
Don't we all agree that tree trunks seem more magnificent
the older they get?
And so it must be true that with our cracks and asymmetrical faces,
our worn skin, weighted bodies, weathered hair, our disproportionate
tops and bottoms, with all of the things that make us wild and old,
that we are a thing of beauty, too.

I don't know much about human biology

but isn't it comforting to know that inside, none of us
are calm, cool, and collected? We're a spiral of cells,
a swirling of veins, a funnel of blood and guts.
Our skeletons are freaky, honestly; our organs squishy,
and I bet we all smell pretty awful under our perfumed skin.
I don't know much about human biology, but it is
kind of comforting to know that inside, we're all a mess.

VI

For our minds

Turns out

The summer my daughter is one,
I shout at my husband in the driveway.
Unabashedly, loudly, cruelly. I float above
my anger, see myself with horns, reckless
and wild. Minutes later, I find my daughter
inside watching television with her cousin.
I scoop her up, bury my face in her sweet-
smelling hair, engulf my niece in my arms.
At night, I cry in the bathroom, salty tears
mixing with hot water from the shower.
Later, I'll apologize, try to understand
all of the things that make me burst,
promise to try harder, mean it.

Turns out, I learn, that none of us are the villain,
the victim, the hero, the saint. We are all our
red hot anger, our cool blue tears, our soothing, our fury,
our love beyond reason, our needs, our grace, our might.

To all of the women I've been before

I am making friends with all of the women I've
been before. Trying, really. I meet her all the time,
all thousands of hers, one for each day I've been
alive. There are times she'll jump out at me from
an old song or a photograph stuck between the pages
of a book. *Remember me?* she'll ask. There are days
I pull her out slowly, watch patiently as she walks
across the tightrope in my mind. Some days she
haunts me. The me who was selfish, the me who was
cruel, who made all the wrong choices. She'll pull
out a lawn chair, refuse to leave. I am trying to let her
stay, trying to make space for her here, trying to build
a home for all of the women I've ever been to live.

Vulnerability is the best host

Vulnerability hosts a party at her home.
There are microwaved snacks and oven-
baked goods, but no one remembers the
food, really. She is wearing . . . something,
of course, but her guests can't recall that
either. She talks gently and honestly about
how hard life can be. How beautiful, too.
She is delighted by everyone, appreciates
the differences in us all. *Oh*, someone murmurs,
this feels nice. At the end of the night, no one
wants to go. They've never felt so at ease,
welcomed, safe. V laughs. *I understand*, she says,
her eyes smiling. *Stay as long as you like.*
You'll always have a soft landing place with me.

Maybe the things we're scared of are really our superpowers.

Having babies after thirty-five.
Crying in public.
Risking a comfortable life for an unexpected one.
Making a mistake, apologizing for it.
Feeling embarrassed, feeling regret.
Revealing to the world that we don't, actually, have it all together.
That we can't, actually, do it all.
Admitting that we're scared or jealous or sad.
Discovering that marriage and parenthood work best
when we work on ourselves.
Asking for help when we need it.
Asking for help so others know that they can ask for it, too.

In London I learned to love myself

Across an ocean from old friends and family,
from men who I thought would fill what was missing,
I spent a year in London courting myself.
How many mornings I learned to wake up and plan a
day I knew would delight me.
How many afternoons spent strolling alone through
city parks, my hand in my hand.
How many times I asked myself
Can I take you to dinner? Buy you a drink at a garden pub?
Can I treat you to coffee, sit by the window at a cozy cafe?
A year I spent learning to ask myself what I needed,
and to find it, all on my own.
A year I thought I spent falling in love with a city,
only to learn, the city helped me to fall in love with myself.

Same

I still haven't figured out how to keep
my shower floor clean or make morning
smoothies or respond to stress calmly.
Same, same, same my friends tell me,
a love note of sorts. Maybe the world
doesn't need us to cut down on carbs or
make more money or waste less time.
Maybe instead it needs us to reach those
who feel alone in their messy homes or
difficult relationships or unresolved
issues. To impress less and connect
more. To share one simple message:
Same. Same, same, same.

June

Every so often I'm convinced I tell the world too much. Hold my heart on my sleeve, cough out my secrets, confess to my pain. I swear to myself I won't do it again, I'll be all lock key, a porch with screens, elusive and safe. Then I talk with a friend who's all heart, all summer and June—raw and flawed but so complete and I'm reminded of how flowers thrive when they're open to it all. To the rain and sun, to footsteps and weeds, to the changing of seasons over again. And when someone's looking for a sign of hope, there they are. Blooming, despite it all.

Until I thought of myself as the sea

I used to separate good days from bad until
I thought of myself as an ocean. I used to
split times I felt strong from when I felt weak
until I imagined myself as the sea. Calm and
rocky, wild and soft, still and powerful and vast
and more than any one thing. In the ocean it's
hard to divorce one mood from another, one wave
from the next. Now, on my worst days, I think
of how good life is too, how I still can greet joy
while swimming through grief. How fragile
strength feels. How I'm not any one thing in any
one moment on any one day. I'm all of it and
all of it is me.

The world is unpredictable and so, often, are my moods

Yesterday I cried about death. The concept of it, anyway.
I felt at odds with the day. It was here and I was there
and everything good felt so sad, too. Even though the sun
was out, even though when you asked me what was wrong
I couldn't say. Today, I sat in the yard with our daughter
and for nearly an hour we listened to the birds and she touched
the grass, then jumped into my lap and I felt happy and
content, but nothing had changed. The world is unpredictable
and so, often, are my moods. And even when I try to change
a bad one to good, sometimes no amount of sunshine will do.
Sometimes, I have to wait for the next day to come and
I'll find myself sitting in damp grass on a cool Monday in
March, seeing it all in bright colors again.

Not therapy, but it just might help

It's not therapy, sitting in the shade
on a restaurant patio at seven PM in June,
flower beds lining the rails, string lights
above you, water in the distance.
Warm air, cool breeze, cold drinks,
bread and oil, olives, cheese, friends
around the table, a small intimate group.
It's not therapy, when you've just ordered
the main course, the appetizers are placed
on the table, someone is telling a story and
you can sit back and laugh.
It's not therapy *(which is wonderful, too)*
but it just might help.

People who annoy us

On our trip, we visit the museum of modern art,
watch as groups of women in their twenties take
countless photos of each other in front of the artwork,
making it nearly impossible to enjoy the exhibits
without disrupting their shoot.
They pose, take pictures, look at the photos on
their phones, switch and repeat.
Model, then photograph, photograph then model.
I launch an irritated inner monologue until
the voice in my head reminds me that this entire trip,
I have been tickling my baby to make her laugh in every
family photograph, immediately looking at the phone to
check that we captured her toothy grin.
And it was humbling, but also comforting to realize that
we're not all that different from the people who annoy us.
Not all that different at all.

(In the best of ways) no one cares what I do

A friend told me she got advice that once people give you
their opinions, no one really spends very much time thinking
about your life at all, not nearly as much as we think they do.
Which feels so freeing in a way. While I'm worried what people
are thinking about the last dumb thing I did or what mistake
I'm about to make, they're consumed with their own decisions.
And what a way to be cared for. To be seen, to be thought of,
to be helped. And then to be released, to go and do what I please.

I want ~~my child~~ to be

a woman who walks among trees like they
are people. Curious, devoted, inquisitive.
Who walks among people like they are trees.
Careful, reverent. Who listens to the words
of a religion that isn't hers and wonders about
how others find meaning. Who sees a stranger
as someone who somebody loves. Who meets
her own shadow and asks it what it needs to grow.
A woman who looks into the bathroom mirror
at a crowded bar one night after dancing for
hours, who sees messy hair and tired eyes,
lipstick teeth and sweat. Who smiles instead
of frowns, who stares her reflection right in
the eyes and says *I love you, I love you,*
I love you the most.

Perspective

In almost every photograph of me and my daughter
from her first two years of life, her expression is
stone-cold serious. In almost every photo I have
that she is pictured without me, she is laughing.
I'm a ball of despair thinking about how she looks
so unhappy with her mother until I realize that in
every picture I am not in, I was behind the camera.
In every picture I am not in, she is smiling right back at me.

Everyone on the internet has it more together than me*

One woman is remodeling her hundred-year home, single-handedly
pulling out baseboards, raising five children and maintaining a full
skincare routine. Another is getting up at four AM to work out,
make eggs and tell you how to grow your hair. Most mornings,
I roll out of bed with my one child, walk down the hall, make coffee,
sit down with her on the floor, curl up under blankets and read.
I lack skills and patience for home improvement, have deprioritized
skin and hair routines for the moment, have deprioritized most things
in lieu of spending time with my baby girl, and while I fear I don't
have it all together, when we're together, I'm certain that I have it all.

---

* or so it seems

How I want this all

The baby screamed the last hour of the road
trip and we pulled over three times in thirty
minutes. By the third, we were blaming each
other and just as we too were about to cry,
we laughed. In the parking lot of an Applebee's
off a highway exit twenty minutes from home,
you walked our daughter up and down under
a warm July sky while I buttoned up my milk-
stained shirt and thought so many things.
Like *I told you so* and *has the crying stopped*
and *I want to be home* and I want so many
things but *how I want this, how I want this,
how I want this all.*

VII

For our children

I forgot to say thank you

In all of my worry I forgot to say thank you.
I worried before because *what if* and
what if not. And then for nine months
straight I worried at least once every day
about the baby, and though that is a
lot of worry, it's no excuse.
I was annoyed because spontaneous
nausea is more romantic in theory.
Exhaustion, too.
I asked you, *why, why, why?*
Why are you tired? Why are you sick?
Even though I knew.
I liked to see you grow and expand
but I wondered why you could not walk
uphill without stopping to rest.
And why did your back ache at night
when we were meant to be hoarding sleep?
In the delivery room I was focused on
the task at hand and you performing it
just right that I forgot then, too.
And after, it was such a blur as you healed
and we became an outside home for an outside baby.
So I forgot until now to say it.
But I would like to.
My body, all of you, every last inch.
Thank you.

The year I became a mother

You won't remember this year when we fell in love.
So quickly, in an instant. How you were born and
the world backed away, gave us space to become.
How those first weeks were like a dream. So delicate,
so fragile, both of us were. How we learned together.
How many hours and days I spent feeding you,
how happy I was to watch you grow. How I held you
close when we walked, taught you about the world.
How you taught me. You won't remember this year.
This year I thought *a mother* was a thing I would
become, *mothering* was a thing I would learn.
How in the end, it turned out to be a thing
I had always been, I had always known.
I was just waiting for you.

My mothering mind is split in half.

One half is logical, practical, sarcastic.
It says things like *I love you kid,*
but I need a break. It gives you
quick hugs, tells you *you're fine!*
when you are crying for me to pick you up.
It sighs when you wake up an hour after bedtime,
right when we're about to watch our show.

The other half is illogical, completely impractical.
It considers homesteading, homeschooling, lies awake
at four AM thinking about how to stay alive forever
so you're never without me. It feels desperate to keep you close,
to never let you out of its sight. It runs to you when you cry,
wants to hold you in its lap all day, cast off all responsibility,
anything in life that isn't you.
It thinks about how its heart has become completely
yours since you were born and I took it out of my body,
handed it straight over to you.

A parent and a child

All my life I have wondered if things are fair.
I know the answer, they are not.
I know I have gotten the long stick of many things.
And still, I pout, even when I step outside of my body,
see myself as a stubborn child unable to recognize compromise,
unable to appreciate the small things, even the big things that are good.
I am caught between a child and a parent all the time.
Being a child with my own. Lying on the floor next to her,
reading a book, spotting a dog. A flower.
Trying my best to parent her and myself, too.
Are you tired? Should you rest? Are you hungry?
Did you eat enough fresh greens? Is this a tantrum?
What do you need? A break, a hug, for someone to hold you?
For someone to show you how kindness looks when you give it to
yourself.

Need

On summer afternoons the year my daughter is one,
I wait for the babysitter to arrive, then close the door
to a room in the small ranch home we are renting.
I try to get everything from the kitchen I will need for
the next few hours—apples, peanut butter, coffee, water,
balance them all in my hands as I walk out of the room for
fear that if I return temporarily, my daughter will cry,
cling to me, lock eyes in a way that will make me feel like crying, too.
I hear her voice in the other room throughout the afternoons,
sometimes laughing, talking, sometimes crying, sometimes saying
Mama, Mama, hoping, maybe, that she will conjure me up.
Or maybe, just a reflex. So many needs she and I have.
I need a snack, to use the bathroom, more water.
I need to write these poems, to finish this book I have started,
to have time alone. I need her to be happy, to feel safe and
loved. She needs me in eyesight, to know I am there.

Our delicate balance of needs feels like a never-ending math
problem. Does she need me more than I need this time?
I try to solve the equation, balance it out, meet our needs in
equal parts, but it never seems to quite work. We are not two
sides of an equation, two values needing to be solved.
We are two people, two separate people, who are desperately
still trying to be one.

New mom friends

It's less that what we used to love
we have in common and more that
we love our children in a way that feels
immeasurable, unconditional, and out of
control, really. It's that no one could warn
us because it's impossible to describe and
now we're here with our hearts having left
our bodies and what can we do, really, other
than lean on each other?

I mean, what can we do, really, other than
to say things like *these crazy babies* and *my gosh,
me too* and *I think it's the hormones* because it's
harder to say that our lives now feel completely
unraveled by overwhelming love. What can we say,
really, other than to make each other laugh and
send memes at midnight and remind one another
that we are *in it* and things will get easier and that
really, the avalanche of fragile love that feels like it
has happened to us and us alone? Well, it's all of us.
It is us all, mothers. We are, indeed, all in this together.

Moms Group

In the moms group we sit in a circle.
Bold women, shy in our new power.
The doula asks us questions, encourages us to share.
Each mom whispers what she fears is her truth alone.
I cry when I speak, not knowing exactly why.
Eight weeks since my daughter has been here
and I think maybe I should have figured it all out.
The babies lie on our chests or on blankets and we ask
questions frantically, like we are trying to excel at
a job for which we have received no training.
Each week for a month we meet, but I can't remember
what we said, only that our heads nodded along,
a chorus of women who understood that it was easier
not to do this alone.

Breastfeeding

The hardest thing about breastfeeding
was not learning to do a new thing
minutes after giving birth,
not the hours that added up to days
that added up to months that I spent
sitting on a bed, in a rocker, on the
couch or the floor, in the car, at the park,
at restaurant tables and on sidewalk
benches feeding my baby. Not the time
I spent with a pump in the middle of
the night, on conference calls,
in hotel rooms. Not the labor of
cleaning bottles and pumping parts,
not the pain of swollen breasts and
infected milk ducts. The hardest part
was learning to be kind to my body,
to be gentle with myself, to block out the *shoulds*,
to listen to my needs, too, to learn how to care for
myself in the same way, with the same love,
that I cared for my child.

At least once a week the plans go awry.

The babysitter's sick, the nap schedule's off,
unexpected rain ruins our chance to go outside,
and I find myself with you, in our small home,
reading the same books. Walking, talking, eating.
Things that only feel like magic when they're first
done. In these days when there's nothing to do,
it feels sacred, this act of parenting. When there
are no photos or applause, just us, in our little house,
learning small things that will become big.
In this time when I am your sun and moon and
you are mine, and it is sacred, me and you.

Surviving is thriving

At the park, she was having so much fun running
and waving hello and playing peek-a-boo that I thought
maybe we could delay the nap and so we did.
When it was time to go, my daughter screamed *EAT*
and pulled my hair like she was trying to yank it out
and hit her small hands against my chest.
I stood in line to get a snack and cold water,
felt my own throat rise in my mouth, sticky and weak,
the hot sun in my face.
Eventually, I found a shady bench to feed her and
our heartbeats slowed down.
Both of us, overstimulated, tearful, in need of rest.
Both of us, thriving.

A village it takes

When I had my daughter I thought I had to be the everything mom. The crafty mom, the sporty mom, the nature mom, the cooking mom, the musical mom, the adventure mom, the gardening mom. It turns out, I'm a little bit of everything, but mostly the *let's get out of the house and socialize* mom, because that's who I have always been, mom or not. And I've found that's good enough. There is a village of people for everything else.

Home maker

I am no good at cooking, cleaning, interior design,
or really, I'm okay at all three. But when my one-year-old
daughter arrives back at the house that we rent,
claps her hands and runs to the toys that sit in the
cozy corner where we spend hours together each week,
when we lean on the windowsill in the living room,
wave to neighborhood dogs walking by, when she jumps
up and down on the couch, flops back in laughter and
ease, I know that she knows, my daughter knows,
that this is her home, and I, her mother, am its maker.

Little moment with little you

In the morning I pour coffee and
sit on the floor next to you.
You bring me stuffed animals
one by one, we give them toy cups
and pretend they are drinking, too.
You hand me books and read your
own, flip through every one in all
of the rows I stacked last night.
I am both delighted and restless and
I am aware, though it is hard to grasp,
that each day you are becoming more
of a person who will one day have
thoughts and dreams that are not
intertwined with mine. And so I drink
my coffee, sit here in this little moment
with little you for the little time we have
on our living room floor when both of us
want to be nowhere else but here.

Twenty years from now I will not remember this hour

that I spent sitting in the car with you while you napped.
February sun pouring in, wrapping around your small sleeping body.
I will remember things as a montage of feelings, a collection of scenes.
How much I ached for time to be mine and still,
how much I hated leaving your side. How things felt relentless.
Caring for something so precious and small. The monotony.
My love for you. Overwhelming, all consuming, relentless.
I'll remember your face, the one that's sleeping less than
a foot away from me right now. I will remember being tired,
when everything was so new. So tired and so in love.

Meals with my daughter

In the morning, I make eggs,
chop cheese, sometimes spinach,
vegan pepperoni I buy in bags.
I sauté it together, butter bread, cut berries in half.
Other days, I spread peanut butter on crackers,
sprinkle Cheerios on your plate, pour coffee for me
and sit on a stool next to your highchair.
I cannot explain why I love watching you eat.
How I find myself staring at you, day after day,
how it almost makes me cry to watch your little hands
pick up food, chew it, swallow.
How happy it makes me to see you enjoy a meal,
how I feel at peace when you are full.

I know we will not always have meals like this,
time like this, a life like this.
I think about days in the future when you may call me as
you are chopping vegetables in your own kitchen,
days that I will hurry through, count the minutes until I can
meet you at a restaurant that you love.

I think even then, I will delight in hearing you
choose items from a menu, in seeing you take bites,
in hearing you say *this food is so good.*

This is the hope of all mothers, I think.
That our children will find joy in filling themselves.
This is the truth of all mothers.
That we will feel peace when our children are full.

Am I doing this right?

My toddler and I want so many of the same things.
To watch unlimited television, to eat frozen pizza
for dinner most nights, to run down the sidewalk,
breeze in our hair, no one holding us back.
But for now, she has found herself a baby,
in need of limits, and I have found myself a mother,
in the business of limiting. So I breathe through
tantrums, hug her small body close, and sometimes,
imagine the day when I will have a child who can
make her own decisions, silently hoping that when
that day arrives, when she is met with so many
choices, she will choose, out of all of them,
to eat frozen pizza and watch television with me.

Being your mother, being your friend

I sit on the floor with you reading books for babies, day after day. I hand you a sippy cup, drink from my coffee mug and we read, sometimes together, the same book, sometimes beside each other, you and I. I imagine us in the future at a coffee shop, sitting at a table, reading our books, me handing you a latte perhaps, drinking my hot coffee with milk, us sharing a scone. Me, reaching across the table to hold your hand or kiss your cheek, and I think about how with all of the things I get to be as your mother, the one that I love most of all is that I get to be your friend.

It all, I think, comes down to friendship.

How much of a friend you are to people you love, to strangers. To the ones who bring you into the world, the ones who care for you, the ones you parent, the ones you share a name with, the ones you date or marry. To yourself. The you who is a wife and mother and sister and daughter and friend. The versions of you from the past, the version of you who is a child, who lives inside you no matter how old you get. It's being a friend to her, loving her, carrying her with you, wherever, however, you go.

Acknowledgments

There are so many people behind this book—people who have directly helped make it a reality, people who are an inspiration for poems, people who give me love and support and help me to do courageous things. I'll try my best to list you all, but if I have forgotten anyone, I am sorry and please know that I am still so very grateful.

A very big thank you to Sarah Cantin for being my fairy godsister of editors. You are a gift and working with you feels like I won the biggest lottery. To so many people at St. Martin's Press, including Jennifer Enderlin, Anne Marie Tallberg, Brant Janeway, Althea Mignone, Rebecca Lang, Alexis Neuville, Chrisinda Lynch, Joy Gannon, Ginny Perrin, Gabriel Guma, Jonathan Bush, and Drue VanDuker. This book would not be a book without you.

To Harriet Prideaux, thank you for making me feel like the luckiest little author and bringing my book to the UK. I am endlessly grateful. To everyone else on the HarperCollins team, including Georgina Atsiaris, Alan Cracknell and Poppy Loughtman—thank you for helping to make my book dreams come true!

To Ariele Fredman, thank you for your always wise guidance and for helping me to get my footing every step of the way. I am so lucky to be able to work with you. To everyone else at United Talent Agency, including Paloma Ortega and Laurie-Maude Chenard, and to Cathryn Summerhayes and Annabel White at Curtis Brown, thank you for being on my team.

To every teacher who has made me feel proud of my work, thank you. Special thanks to John Casteen, whose poetry writing workshop I took one summer gave me all the confidence to believe I could be a poet.

To everyone who follows @hannahrowrites on Instagram and makes me feel like my writing matters. Thank you. If I never get to tell you this in person, just know that you have helped to make my dreams come true.

To my friends. I couldn't ask for better people to share my life with. Thank you for filling my days with so much joy, support, laughter, and love.

To Nanna and Pa, who made me feel like anything I did was wonderful, who instilled in me confidence as a little girl that has stayed with me my whole life. Everyone should have grandparents like you.

To my in-laws, who support me like I am truly their daughter, thank you.

To my siblings. My sisters, who fight out loud with me then laugh out loud with me in a way that only sisters can—thank you for making me feel like I always belong. To my brother-in-law and sister-in-law, thank you for adopting me as one of your own.

To my nieces and nephews, thank you for making my heart grow a million times over.

To my extended family, my aunts and uncles and cousins—thank you for making me feel surrounded by support. There is no better feeling than being part of a family who love each other.

To my parents, who have the biggest book collection I have ever seen. Thank you for always making reading seem fun.

To my mother, who never belittled my dreams, who never told me to be "more realistic," who has always made me feel like I could do anything and be anything.

ACKNOWLEDGMENTS | 219

To my daughter, for giving me the gift of being your mother. It has split me wide open in the best of ways and for that I am forever grateful. You are mine and I am yours, forever.

To Nikhil. Thank you for helping me to be bold and to chase my dreams. Thank you for your steady love. I've heard a soulmate is someone who challenges you to be the best version of yourself. You are mine.

And thank you to all of the younger versions of me, all thousands of her. For being brave even when you were scared. For looking for joy even when you felt sad. For walking forward even when you felt like crumbling. Thank you.

About the Author

Maria Silva-Goyo

Hannah Rosenberg is a poet whose work has been shared widely online, and she has been featured in publications serving women and parents like *Darling* and *In Kind*. She lives in the greater Philadelphia area with her husband and daughter, who often find themselves the subjects of her poems. You can find her work on Instagram @hannahrowrites.